WHEN PUSH COMES TO LOVE

From **REJECTION** to **REJOICING**

A Christian mothers relationship with her gay daughter

By: Becky A. Davis

From Rejection to Rejoicing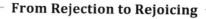

Copyright©2014 Becky A. Davis

When Push Comes To Love:
From rejection to rejoicing
A Christian mother relationship with her gay daughter.

ISBN-13: 978-1497329935
ISBN-10: 1497329930

All rights reserved. No part of this book may be reproduced or transmitted in any form or by any means electronic or mechanical, including photocopying, recording, or by any information storage and retrieval system without the written permission of the author, except where permitted by law.
Printed in the United States of America

When Push Comes To Love

TABLE OF CONTENTS

Dedication ……………………………………………….4

Introduction ……………………………………………..5

Chapter 1 - The Trick: Satan's Tactics ……………27

Chapter 2 – The Fight: Spiritual Warfare…………56

Chapter 3 – The Work: Submission to God ……..76

Chapter 4 – The Change: Spirit Comforts ……….94

Chapter 5 – The Challenge: Self or Savior ……..107

90-day Love Push Challenge ……………………...114

Join the Conversation ……………………………...179

DEDICATION

This book is dedicated to my daughter, Jasmine
Our relationship has helped
Me to be a better Christian
Which helped me to be a better mother.

I wouldn't change a thing
Because I learned how
To love.

I love the relationship God has
Given us and I pray that he gives
Us many more years to
Keep making it better and better.

INTRODUCTION

*So now faith, hope and love abide, these three;
but the greatest of these is LOVE.
I Corinthians 13:13*

Love, has been described as the greatest gift of all. In the scripture above the bible also calls love the greatest.

We all want love and to be loved. It sounds like a simple thing to do yet loving unconditionally is one of the hardest things to do. You see, we all put conditions on our love, yet we don't often see the conditions we add to loving someone. When you think about your spouse or someone you love and have to describe why you love them, most people name things that they do like, " he is considerate," "she supports me," "he's a good kid," "she's never given me any problems."

If the person you loved stopped doing these things, does your love stop? Your love may not stop but unfortunately we start to show love in an unloving ways.

From Rejection to Rejoicing

In the book Love Dare by Steven and Alex Kendrick, it states " love is not determined by the one being loved, but rather by the one *choosing* to love." That statement really messed with me and caused me to think. It was a mind changing statement for me.

HOW DID THIS BOOK ORIGINATE?

So many churches are not addressing homosexuality, yet so many families are dealing with it and struggling with how to deal family members who are homosexual.

I have shared my story in parts when I have spoken at churches or inspirational ladies day programs and I realize that so many people are hurting *and* they are hurting their loved ones who's gay, because they are confused with what to do. In my experience, I have found that a lot of Christian's do what comes easy when it comes to homosexuality, ignore it, judge it, and don't speak of it. I know this to be true because I did this myself. We need to start a healthy conversation to bring together Christians to help them understand what God has called us to do.

Love.

I had an awakening regarding my on-going struggle with my relationship with my daughter. There were so many things that affected our relationship and this one issue almost changed our relationship forever, until I **chose to love** no matter what. See, I struggled to do what I was suppose to do as a Christian. I knew what the bible said about loving one another, at least I thought I knew. As a Christian, the bible teaches in Ephesians 5:1-2, "Be imitators of God, as beloved children and walk in Love just as Christ also loved you." Let's just say I did not imitate God well and did not show the same love that Christ showed me to my daughter.

From Rejection to Rejoicing

MY STORY

I found out in my daughter's ninth grade high school year that she was interested in dating women.

Jasmine, I will use her name because she authorized me to do so, had gotten in trouble for something, I can't even remember what it was but she was on punishment. I had taken her cell phone from her for two weeks. On the day I was going to give it back to her, a small voice said, check to see who she had been talking to. That was a mother's instinct. I turned the phone on and started looking at her incoming calls and out going calls and nothing seem strange or out of place. Then I opened her text messages to see who and what she was texting. I started reading messages that was clearly someone she was interested in. I was trying to figure out who this person was because of course the name was coded. As I continued to read, my stomach dropped and my eyes popped as wide as they could go and my heart started racing fast. There was a text she wrote that stated how much she liked a girl she went to school with. In the text she used the name and not the "coded" name.

When Push Comes To Love

I think I fell to the floor. I didn't want to read anymore but I could not put it down. I sat there and matched up the text from what Jasmine wrote and what the responder wrote and the picture was getting clearer and clearer.

"My daughter is GAY!" My heart was crushed and broken.

I could not wait until she came home from school, because I needed to understand this. Maybe someone used her phone at school. I told myself a hundred different reasons why the texts were in her phone. That day it took forever for school to end, I'm sure it was because I could not wait. I prayed so hard, "God please don't let his be."

When she came home from school, I sat her down and as calmly as I could, because I did not want her to lie to me or feel she can't tell me and I knew if I started out mad, yelling and screaming, she would not tell me. So my plan was to remain calm no matter what she told me.

We sat down and I asked her, "Jasmine, who do you like at school?" she said, "no one really." I

From Rejection to Rejoicing

asked, "What about Sam?" the boy she liked the previous year and she said, "no I don't like him anymore." I said to her, "I know you like somebody," by then she had a feeling I knew more than I was letting on and of course she was right. She looked at me, and I could see that she wanted to say something but was holding it back. I said to her, "tell me Jasmine" she said, "yes, I do like someone, but you won't like them." I said, "how do you know that?', she took her time and I could see her fear appear and nervousness, then she said, "because it's a girl."

I sat there still, replaying in my head what I thought I just heard. My heart was pounding in my chest and I could see she was scared and surprised that she said it out loud and that she had said it to me.

I was surprised that I was still calm at least on the outside because inside I was slowing dying, but I wanted to know more. I asked her about the girl and how long she has liked her and she said that it had just been a few months. The more we talked about it I found out that it was a girl in her youth group at church. At CHURCH! What?

When Push Comes To Love

How could this be? I was devastated and broken inside.

I asked her, "do you think this is right in the eyes of God?" she said, "no." "Do you know what the bible says about homosexuality?" I asked, she said, "I know it's wrong, but I like her."

Let me tell you, I didn't know what to do, how to have a conversation. I was lost.

I had to figure out how to tell my husband and Jasmine's father. Jasmines dad and I divorced when she was almost five. I remarried when she was in the eight-grade. We had a blended family. My husband had three kids and I had one, so we were raising four kids together but Jasmine was the only one who lived in the home with us.

My husband and I had only been married a year or so at this point and we were already having issues in our marriage adjusting to living together and how to raise kids, and I knew this was not going to be easy.

From Rejection to Rejoicing

I called my husband, because he was working out of town, to tell him about the conversation I had with Jasmine and he was shocked. He called her and started asking her question after question until she was exhausted. He was clearly upset about it too.

I called her father who lived in Nebraska to let him know and he wanted to talk to her, I gave her the phone and he asked her question after question and told her how wrong it was.

Looking back on it that was a tough day for us all but Jasmine was hit the hardest from her parents and we were all exhausted. Everyone was calm that day just hurt and frustrated by the end of that first day, but the worst was yet to come.

Jasmine told me that she would end the relationship. Great, we thought. As time went on I realized that it had not stopped. I was in her room and found a letter she had written to a girl about them hooking up. Now, I was mad. She told us that, just to calm us down and keep the peace, but her intention was to continue what she was doing in secret.

From that point on everything that she did was magnified in my eyes. If she got in trouble at school, I magnified it because I knew she liked girls. If she got home late, I magnified it because I knew she liked girls and she must have been with one to be late. I was so upset I started pushing her away, not realizing it. If she got a phone call, I assumed it was some girl she liked and I got upset and was mad at her the whole day. At that time, I didn't realize what I was doing to her. I was stuck on how it affected me.

My husband could not take it. It caused us so many problems. He distanced himself away from her and I could see it and it hurt me because, remember we are a blended family and "my" daughter was embarrassing us both. The crazy thing is I did not want him to treat her any different, but I was treating her different. As a mother you can be upset with your child and say things that are hurtful, but you never want to hear someone else say things to hurt your child. Of course I was just as wrong but I couldn't see it in me but I could see it in others.

From Rejection to Rejoicing

Jasmine had started coming into our room and sneaking my husband's clothes to wear to school. She would leave the house in one outfit and change into men clothing when she got to school. My husband started finding his pants and shorts in her room. My husband was a size 38 and Jasmine was a size 5 in junior sizes, which means the clothes were huge on her. That's when I found out that she felt more comfortable in men's clothes than women's cloths. I got mad all over again.

That night I cried and I cried. How could my daughter "want" to wear men clothes, I said to myself over and over. I could not get my head wrapped around it. It made no sense to me. My daughter wants to look like a guy. I cannot tell you the pain I felt from that. It's not enough that she liked girls but now she want to look like the guy in the relationship.

This crushed me more than finding out she was gay. As you read further you will find out why.

Jasmine was a daddy's girl. She has always been her daddy's girl because he loved her and because he would let her have her way and I was the disciplinarian who would say no candy, no ice cream, or just say no. He never could say no to her or should I say rarely said no to her. Her father and I had different views raising children.

I always made sure that she had a relationship with her dad and that she saw him as much as he wanted because I did not have that kind of relationship with my dad, I wanted my child to have a relationship with her dad. I never wanted her to live with him because I wanted her raised in church and he was not going to church and he drank too much alcohol for me. I did not want her to live everyday in that environment but I did want her to have a close relationship with him.

Jasmine would say, from the time she was five, "can I stay with dad," it would break my heart but I would have to say, "no baby, you can visit him but you have to stay with me."

After two years of battling this issue of her being gay, I decided to let her move to another state, Nebraska, with her dad. I knew it was not the right thing to do but I was ashamed, embarrassed and hurt. I thought if I can't see what she is doing, it would be better for me of course. Our relationship was getting worse and worse. We loved each other, but we did not like each other. I did not make that decision for the right reasons, and I knew it, but I was thinking about ME.

I cried for months after she left, so much so that my husband said, "You have to stop doing this. Everyday you are sad and crying and I don't know what to do." I missed her and I realized later that I was crying because I knew I should have not sent her away. I missed her so much that it hurt. I should have faced it and my guilt was eating me up.

We went through five years of a bitter relationship, because of her lifestyle, at least that's what I thought before I realized that it was my *choice* that impacted how I showed love to her.

I finally made a decision to stop shoving her and to just love her and our relationship changed in ways that I could not imagine. My belief was that if she changed, our relationship would be better but God was teaching me that I needed to change. You see, Ephesians 3:20 states, "Now unto him who is able to do exceeding abundantly above all that we ask or think, according to the power that works in us." I was not using my spiritual power, just my hurt, pain, anger and shame.

I finally shared my story of how God taught me how to focus on love and not the lifestyle of my daughter being gay during a Sunday school class at church. I couldn't believe what I was saying out loud for the first time and of course many were shocked to hear it. There were so many people that approached me to tell me that they too had someone in their family that was gay and how it was disrupting their family.

As God worked on me and begin to change me, my relationship with my daughter changed. When I focused on what God was teaching me, I realized it was I he was teaching all the time. I wanted him to teach Jasmine, but the lesson was for me.

From Rejection to Rejoicing

I proudly called myself a Christian; yet I did not demonstrate the most important commandment, LOVE. I realized that all the other stuff I did in church was nothing if I could not love and show love.

I could show love to everyone else, but my daughter was missing the love of her mother. I use to say, I love everyone, but God showed me that I was a liar. I was a fraud. I was a hypocrite. I realized that God loves me enough to reveal me to me. I cried again because I did not like what I saw in myself as a Christian and especially as a mother.

I could not see it and I would not have seen it because I felt I was a good person and living an honest life tying to live Christ-like. God challenged me to stop talking about his word and start living his word. I repented for those sins.

When I opened up and started sharing my story, I was surprised by the amount of people that had this same issue. As I have talked to people, I could see their hurt and I saw myself in them. I realized that so many Christian struggled with loving homosexuals especially in their family.

MY BELIEF

Let me be clear in my belief, I believe homosexuality is a sin, because the bible says that it is a sin. I Corinthians 6:9-10, *"Or do you not know that wrongdoers will not inherit the kingdom of God? Do not be deceived: neither the sexually immoral, nor idolaters, nor adulterers, nor men who have sex with men, nor thieves, not the greedy, nor drunkards, nor slanderers, nor swindlers will inherit the kingdom of God."* (NIV)

Romans 1: 26-27, *"For this reason, God gave them up to shameful lusts. Even their women exchanged natural sexual relations for unnatural ones. In the same way men also abandoned natural relations with a women and were inflamed with lust for one another. Men committed shameful acts with other men, and received in themselves the due penalty for their error."* (NIV)

These scriptures describe how people who commit these acts without repentance will not see

God. I didn't say those words, *God said those words*, and I just repeated them. If you get mad reading this book, don't' be mad at me be mad at God.

PURPOSE OF THIS BOOK

This book is not to argue if homosexuality is right or wrong, I have already clearly stated my belief.

If you get caught up being focused on homosexuality being right or wrong you will miss the purpose of this book.

This book is to show you how to stop **Pushing and Shoving** and start **Pushing and Loving.** We can disagree with one another and still show love. We should not have to scream, fuss and fight and turn our back on someone because they think and feel differently than we do. Love covers a multitude of sins.

I realized that *God has a bigger plan for our problems and our problems have a bigger purpose.* My past situation was divinely arranged to help someone else with a present situation. I am so thankful to God for the experience, because it drew me closer to him, which drew me close my daughter.

I will share with you my journey and how God showed me that I was talking and not walking.

WHAT ARE THE BENEFITS OF THIS BOOK?

If you have someone in your family or a close friend that's living a lifestyle that you disagree with, this book will help you strengthen your spiritual relationship with God, which will change every relationship you have.

This book is for Christians who struggle with other people's life decisions as a gay person. For Christian believers we are commanded to love. If you are not a Christian, you are not under this command from God. John 13:34 - "A new commandment I give unto you, that ye love one another; as I have loved you that ye also love one another. By this shall all men know that ye are my disciples, if you have love one to another."

From Rejection to Rejoicing

(NIV) I can truly say that as a Christian my daughter did not see me as a disciple of Christ, all she saw was a hurt, and an angry mother, and not much love.

My prayer is for you to move beyond talking about love and start acting in love. Not just to the people that make it easy for you to love, but for those that present a challenge. I pray that you measure yourself by God's word and not by how you feel because how we feel and what God's word says might not be the same and often times don't line up.

I want to share with you what I have learned in the hopes that it blesses you and your relationships with others and that it draws you nearer to God.

So many Christians struggle, just like I did, when they have someone in their family that is gay, homosexual, lesbian or how ever you want to say it.

We as Christians struggle with loving, gay people more than the world, but the world will show love and too many Christians do not. We set our selves above everyone else with a holier than thou attitude, but Jesus did not show us that example. Not every Christian handles homosexuality badly. There are so many that are grounded in God's plan and his word and love and pray their way through the hurt and pain and if that is you, then this book is not for you but if that is not you, please read on. My prayer is that this book helps as many people as possible, especially Christians, since God has commanded us to LOVE. Love works. It is a powerful motivator and it always does what is best for others. It is the strength needed for us to face our greatest problems.

WHAT'S THE BEST WAY TO USE THIS BOOK?

My prayer is that you will find this book full of "ah-ha" moments along with ideas that can fast-forward your relationships with others and draw you nearer to God. I pray that your heart is touched in a way that caused you to change how you show love one to another.

Based on a new report on CBS in Atlanta in November 2012, 40% of homeless youths are LGBT (Lesbian, Gay, Bi-sexual, or Transgender) and have been kicked out by their families and or disowned. 58% become sexually assaulted while on the streets and 62% commit suicide. Not all of those households are Christian homes but over 80% of Americans claim to be Christian so those numbers are scary and that means that some of those household were Christians that put their children out for being gay.

Please think of your personal situations and how you can apply what you read in this book to your life. What do you want the people you love most to know about you? Do you want them to know that you love them no matter what, or you love them only if?

In chapter one, **THE TRICK**: Satan's Tactics. You will learn how Satan can trick you to easily fall pray to his schemes.

In chapter two, **THE FIGHT**: Spiritual Warfare. You will learn how to fight the devil and not the person.

In chapter three, **THE WORK:** Submit to God. You will learn how to live a life of love. You will understand how to move beyond talking about being a Christian and start walking as a Christian.

In chapter four, **THE CHANGE**: Spirit's Comfort. You will find comfort in the scriptures and strengthen your belief in God's promises.

In chapter five, **THE CHALLENGE:** Self or Savior. Take the 90-day challenge to Push Love and you have to decide what's most important to you, pleasing yourself or the savior.

At the end of each chapter there are reflection questions. Do the work. Take some time to answer those questions, and then take a few minutes to pray.

The questions will help you see who you really are if you are honest with yourself.

From Rejection to Rejoicing

My prayer is that you heal yourself so you can heal your relationships. We all know that hurt people hurt people but healthy people heal people.

Are you ready to move from Shoving to Loving?

Let's jump in.

CHAPTER 1

THE TRICK
Satan's Tactics

THE TRICK
Satan's Tactics

"The thief only comes to steal, kill and destroy." John 10:10 (ESV)

Let me say that Satan had me tricked. He had my thoughts and my actions. And he did it based on my emotions. There are five emotions that Satan used to keep me distracted from love, they were shame, guilt, hurt, anger and embarrassment. Does that sound familiar to you?

If this is a new situation for you, you will feel some if not all of these emotions that will be discussed further in this chapter. If you have been dealing with this situation for some time, you have already felt these emotions.

Each one of these emotions damaged my relationship with my Jasmine. Satan was stealing, killing and destroying my relationship and I didn't even see it because I was too focused on each one of these emotions.

Darkness blinds understanding so you can't grasp the meaning of a message. Let me tell you, I was blinded. As a Christian, Jesus represents the light and Satan represents darkness. There was no light shinning in me when it came to my relationship with Jasmine. I had allowed darkness to take up residence.

John 12:2 - *"During the supper, when the devil had already put it into the heart of Judas Iscariot, Simon's son, to betray him. Satan had planted evil in Judas' heart to betray Jesus."* Judas was not the only one the devil used. He did it to me too and I easily fell into it because of all the negative emotions I felt. Satan is busy on his job and he does it well.

Love must be to Christians what hate is to Satan, a driving force for all actions.

Logic makes you think and emotions make you act. I was not thinking logically because I was caught up in my emotions. I believe that logical decisions are sound decisions and emotional decisions without any logic are usually the wrong decisions.

The first step in any healing and recovery program is to admit that *you* have to change *you*. As long as you make the broken relationship about the other person, true healing cannot happen. This book is about you, not someone else.

SHAME

The definition of shame is the painful feeling arising from the consciousness of something dishonorable, improper or ridiculous that could be done by oneself or another; disgrace.

I felt shame because of how being gay is perceived by people in the church. I did not want anyone to know about Jasmine. I did not tell my mother for a while because I did not want anyone to pull away from Jasmine or treat her different. I know that sounds crazy, when you are doing what you do not want anyone else to do. Again, as a mother, I did not want anyone to hurt my child. All I could think about was what would my family and friends think about *me* with my daughter being gay. Did you hear what I said, I was thinking about me a lot more than the issues and feelings my daughter was having.

Once I found out, I did not want anyone else to know. I was ashamed of her and of course I did not want the people in the church to know. How would they view *me* if they knew? (The trick) Would they start judging me? So what did I do? I did not tell anyone. My husband and I spoke to the other girl's parents about it only because they were experience the same thing and my husband and I thought if the parents could stop their daughter, it would help us with Jasmine. Again, all you can hear is shame in my thinking.

Satan had me so entangled in how I looked that I did not take the time to look into my daughters feeling and thoughts and honestly, I didn't want to understand them.

I remember the day I finally called to tell my mother. It was hard for me. I said, "Mom, I have to tell you something." She said, "What?" "Jasmine is interested in other girls." She didn't get upset or react the way I expected, she just said, "We need to pray for her." She could hear the hurt in my voice and the disappointment and she just said, "It's going to be alright." I really needed to hear that but I didn't quite believe it at the time. We never talked about it again for years.

I was so relieved that my mother who has been in church her entire life did not freak out. At least not on the outside.

I was not the only one ashamed, my husband and our son was ashamed. My husband started to distance himself from her. When I had to work on the weekends, they would get up and go to breakfast or he would take to lunch, dinner or a movie. All that stopped when we found out she was gay. He stopped taking her out, unless he had to, before he did it because he wanted to.

Jasmine and my son attended the same school and he saw her get to school and change clothes and he would just keep his distance from her. Before, they would talk and hang out at school but he was ashamed too.

When Push Comes To Love

His friends were asking him questions about his sister, and of course you know teenagers, they made jokes and he would just laugh it off. I asked him how he felt about it and he said it was embarrassing to him.

Jasmine moved back to live with us her senior year. I had missed her so much and couldn't wait to have her home again. She had been gone a year and it was killing me inside for her to be away. I was so excited; I hated her being away especially in another state.

We were moving from Dallas to Atlanta because I was promoted on my job and I thought, great, we get a new start. I told Jasmine that no one knows about everything that has happen in Texas, so you can make a clean start.

We got to Atlanta and found a great church to make our home and it was a couple months into her senior year that, it started up again. I knew it was not going to stop. I was ashamed again and I couldn't take it. One night she stole my company car and went to meet some girl she liked and I was furious. I decided to send her to her father's again all because I did not want anyone in Atlanta to know and she was getting out of hand with the stunts she was pulling.

After Christmas break, I sent her to Nebraska to live with her dad to finish the last semester of high school.

Shame is one of the root causes of dysfunctional families. It is a powerful, painful and potentially dangerous emotion, especially those who don't understand its origin or know how to manage it. In Genesis 2:25, "Adam and Eve were in the garden and they were naked and not ashamed." But when you get to Genesis 3:10 Adam told God, "I heard the sound of you in the garden, and I was afraid, because I was naked, and I hide myself." Go back to the definition of shame. It was Adam's conscious because he did something dishonorable that made him hide himself.

I was ashamed because Jasmine was doing something dishonorable and I felt it was a disgrace to my family, and me so I hid it. **(The trick)**

When Push Comes To Love

In 2010, there was breaking news of a college male freshman who committed suicide after his roommate used a hidden camera to stream live images of him having sex over the internet with another man. The shame was too much for him to bear. When I saw that on the news, I thought of his parents and I asked myself, "would I rather have her gay or dead?" The answer was easy, of course I want my child alive, even if it meant alive and gay. You have to ask yourself that same question because it forces you to go deeper within yourself.

When we feel shame it's about who we are. That's where shame lives, in our ego. What she was doing, I felt, was about who I was, not who she was. **(The trick)** I really want you to see that it's really more about you than it is about the other person. When we focus on the situation we can't see what God is trying to teach us.

She has always been a fun loving person who's full of jokes. She thinks she is a comedian and actually she is quite funny. When we used to visit friends and family, everyone wanted to see Jasmine because she was a good person to be around. Satan tricked me into not seeing who I knew her to be and I was a willing participant. I allowed it.

Does any of this sound familiar to you? Maybe not the same behaviors, but what about the feeling of shame? Have you been tricked with shame?

My shame caused me to **SHOVE** her away.

GUILT

The definition of guilt is, "a feeling of responsibility or remorse for some offense, crime, wrong, etc. whether real or imagined.

I know this feeling well: guilt. It has followed me during the day and kept me awake at night. I've struggled to get past the things I've done or not done, no matter how much I try.

This is another emotional tactic that Satan used very skillfully on me. As a mother, I questioned,

When Push Comes To Love

"What did I do to contribute to her decision." I felt like I was responsible for her actions and the guilt weighed heavy on me.

Anytime you feel guilt, it's about something you did, where shame is about something you or someone else does. I was searching my mind to recount what could I have done. I realized that the year before I found out she was gay that she was talking about several of her basketball teammates being gay and she would tell us things that they were doing. Well, I just chalked it up as small talk when I should have been listening enough to read between the lines. She was checking to see what my reaction would be. I never took the time to talk to her about that lifestyle and that's where my guilt took over.

Why didn't I ask more questions? Why didn't I ask her what she thought about it? Why did I ignore the topic? I asked myself all these questions and each question made me feel like a horrible mother. I felt I had let my child down.
(The trick)

From Rejection to Rejoicing

I have never and will never claim to be the best mother and probably would not win a best mother award because I have fallen short so many times.

I can say that I have always done the best with what I knew. Unfortunately, I did not know a lot about parenting or homosexuality and she was my only child. I felt guilty for divorcing her dad because maybe she would have been more stable with both of her parents. I felt guilty because I remarried and she wanted me to be with her dad. You name it, I thought about it. I beat myself up over and over again. Satan was working overtime on me.

I raised my daughter in church just like I was raised in the church. One Sunday our minister started a new series called "How to Parent a Prodigal." That series of messages helped me to let go of the guilt I felt. One of the things that Bro Emmanuel White shared was Luke 2:45, when Mary and Joseph could not find Jesus for three days, and when they found him he was in the temple, sitting among the teachers listening to them and asking questions. Mary and Joseph had not done anything wrong for Jesus to walk off and they lost track of him.

So why do we beat ourselves up because of a decision our children makes. Satan tricked me and wanted me to believe that it was my fault.

When you spend days and hours living in your guilt, it's hard to see realistically. Mark 11:25, *"And when ye stand praying, forgive, if ye have ought against any: that your Father also which is in heaven my forgive you your trespasses."* When you feel guilty, you have an ought with yourself and the first step to move beyond the guilt is to forgive yourself for what you have done and for what you think you *should* have done. It's time to forgive yourself to move past guilt.

What you don't want is to feel the guilt of losing a loved one and you did not mend or attempt to mend the relationship. You do not want to stand before God and give an account that you *chose* not to show love towards someone, at least I didn't.

My guilt caused me to **SHOVE** her away.

HURT

The definition of hurt is "to affect adversely; to cause mental pain to; offend or grieve; to suffer want or need.

I was mentally hurt because of her actions and decisions. As I stated earlier, "hurt people hurt people and healthy people heal people." Well, I was hurt and believe me I caused more hurt to her.

I argued about everything she did, from cleaning the kitchen to picking out clothes to wear. I acted from my hurt and it was hurtful. The sad part is that at that time I didn't realize what I was doing. It became a normal part of my interaction with her.

I thought if I show my hurt, it would force her to change. **(The trick)** All it did was make her not want to be around me so she did not have to feel like she is hurting her mother. Once she moved with her father, she stayed away, thinking that it would help the situation because she did not want to see the look in my eyes when I saw her dressed like a guy. I wanted to see her and be around her but I had not let the hurt go.

Jasmine is a funny and loving person. She has always been and my hurt clouded my vision of her. She is a caregiver, she always took care of me and I took care of her because it was she and I for so long. I remember one time when she was about seven or eight years old and I had the flu. I had just enough energy to take her to school and pick her up, and then I would get on the couch and sleep. I would put her toys out and turn the TV on and say mommy is sick and I have to lie down. She was so concerned about me. I used to make her hot tea when she was not feeling well. As I lay on the couch in and out of consciousness due to the medication, she came next to me with a hot cup of tea. I was shocked, because I had not showed her how to make tea, nor did I let her mess with the stove. She said, "I watch you all the time, I know how to do it and I know how to make it taste good with sugar." She had put a cup of hot water in the microwave and added a tea bag. All I could do is smile. Satan trapped me in my hurt and pain so I could not see the love my child had for me.

When Jesus hung on the cross, after being beaten, spit on, hit, hands nailed, feet nailed, stabbed in his side, thorns mashed down on his head, he looked at the people who had done this to him and said, "Father forgive them, for they know not what they do." - Luke 23:34. I cry now as I write this because of His love for me and my lack of love towards my daughter at that time. He loved me in spite of me, it's the least I could have done for Jasmine. (Thank you God for forgiving me)

Through His hurt, He still loved us. This is our example of how we should love. Following Jesus is not about trying, it's about dying to self. We must die to ourselves daily.

My hurt caused me to **SHOVE** her away.

ANGER

The definition of anger is, "a strong feeling of displeasure and belligerence aroused by a wrong; wrath.

This was the emotional tactic that Satan used to fuel the other three emotions. He kept me in an angry state for four years. Psalms 4:4 states, "be angry, and do not sin; ponder in your own hearts on your beds, and be silent." I will tell you this, I was angry and I sinned in my words to her, my actions, my behavior and most of all towards God.

I believed that if I showed her love that it meant that I accepted her choice. **(The trick)** I loved my daughter but I did not do a good job of *showing* it to her. I really, really believed this trick. Many of you probably believe this too.

You believe that your anger will change something and that will work in your favor.

From Rejection to Rejoicing

I did not want to talk to her about it, unless she was telling me that she was done with that life. When I did talk to her about it, it was to show her how wrong it was. I used the bible as a weapon on her. And we wonder why people don't come back to the church. You can't beat up a person and believe that they are going to embrace the beating. It's not in our nature as human beings.

Survival instincts teach us to protect ourselves when we feel threaten or hurt. As a Christian, I had given Satan so much power in my thoughts and actions. Does any of this sound familiar to you?

I was listening to Oprah radio and Iyanla Fix My Life was on talking to a girl who was going through the process to change her sexuality to become a man. Her father, who was a Christian and a pillar in the church, did not accept her choice and refuse to deal with his daughter. He had rejected his daughter. His daughter wanted the love of her father so bad. You could hear the hurt in her voice and she shared how much she wanted a relationship with her father. When the father was interviewed you could also hear the hurt in his voice of her lifestyle. So who should change?

Here is the answer, the one who want to be able to share with God in the judgment that they did the right thing. Hebrews 9:27 says, "And as it is appointed unto men once to die, but after this the judgment."

What do you want to share with God during that conversation? This question really helped me to change my behavior and my thinking.

The word love is in the bible over 440 times, and anger is there 28 times, yet we focus on being upset and mad without the presence of love. I focused on the 28 instead of the 440.

Jasmine is not a person that holds on to anger. If she get's upset she can let it go quickly. She did not get that trait from me; it's something I needed to learn from her. She could do something and get in trouble and lose her privileges and the next day wake up like nothing ever happened. There were lessons that she was teaching me and I didn't even realize it until later.

I let my anger **SHOVED** her away.

EMBARRASSED

The definition of embarrassed is, to make uncomfortably, self-conscious; disconcert; abash.

My daughter's lifestyle made me uncomfortable, so I was embarrassed. When you are embarrassed it will change your actions.

Of course, everyone in the family was embarrassed. We did not talk about what was going on in our house to anyone because we were all embarrassed.

We took a family trip with all of the kid to the Dominican Republic. Everyone was an adult except our youngest daughter. Our son didn't get his passport in time so he wasn't able to go. We were all excited and couldn't wait to hang out.

My husband said that he wanted to dance with all his girls when we got there. I thought that was so sweet. After getting there and seeing Jasmine and they way she dressed, masculine, he changed his mind. He asked our oldest daughter to dance, but didn't ask Jasmine. I knew why, but I felt he should have done what he said. But he was embarrassed. Like most people, we wonder what others will think.

On that vacation the girls stayed away from Jasmine. At home they were ok but in public, they were embarrassed. I asked them to find out what made them embarrassed and it was that someone might mistake them as being her girlfriend because they don't know they are sisters.

I understood that but at the same time, I knew it was hurtful to Jasmine.

Embarrassment is considered one of the self-conscious emotions, quite at ease in the company of guilt, shame, and pride. Given that embarrassment happens in relation to other people, it is a public emotion that makes you feel exposed, awkward, and filled with regret for whatever you or someone else's wrongdoing happens to be. Potential negative evaluations concerning standards about actions, thoughts, and feelings that govern our behavior are at the core of embarrassment and other self-conscious emotions (Lewis, 2008).

The experience of embarrassment alerts you to your failure to behave according to certain social standards, which threaten the beliefs you hold concerning how others evaluate you as well as the ways in which you evaluate yourself.

Embarrassments usually result from accidental behaviors that lead you to feel negatively about yourself--even when you had no intention of violating a social standard.

I know that I'm not the only person who has been in this situation and felt embarrassed.

CHAPTER SUMMARY

Be Aware of Satan's Tricks

When Push Comes To Love

John 10:10 - *"The thief cometh not, but for to steal, and to kill and to destroy: I come that they might have life and that they might have it ore abundantly."* This scripture helped me to begin to *see* Satan's tactics. He wanted to steal my relationship with my daughter, he wanted to kill our love for each other and he wanted to destroy my relationship with God. What is he doing in your relationship?

Satan seeks to ruin your relationships. As Christian's, be aware of his tricks, schemes and tactics.

1 John 4:20 - If anyone says, *"I love God, yet hates his brother, he is a liar. For anyone who does not love his brother, whom he has seen, cannot love God, whom he has not seen."* (NIV) This scripture should speak to your spirit. I loved Jasmine but I did not show love, which is what this scripture is talking about. Anytime you withhold love, you are breaking God's most important commandment. Matthew 22:38-39, says, *"Jesus said unto him, Thou shalt love the Lord thy God with all they heart, and with all they soul, and with all they mind. This is the first and*

great commandment. And the second is like unto it, Thou shall love they neighbor as thyself. On these two commandments hang all the law and the prophets."

As a Christian you and I are commanded to love and to love others over ourselves.

If you are holding love back from someone, it's time for you to fix it, while you still have time.

If you have felt any of these emotions they are real emotions. My prayer is that you channel those emotions to act in love. Don't do what I did. Please don't let years go by like I did before you get it. Get your emotions in check or Satan will have a field day in your mind.

THE ULTIMATE LOVE STORY

The Passion of Jesus Christ is the greatest love story ever told and it's true. Jesus said in John 10:18, "No one takes My life, but I gladly lay it down on My own initiative…"

Jesus did not "Make the ultimate sacrifice." Jesus WAS the ultimate sacrifice! That's LOVE.

He gave his life to save our lives and he says to you today, "Bring Me your sin, and I will bring you My righteousness. Bring Me your sickness, and I will bring you My health. Bring Me your lack, and I will bring you My provision. Bring Me your confusion, and I will bring you My peace. Bring Me your depression, and I will bring you My joy. Bring Me your hate and I will bring you my Love"

Jesus gave so many examples of "showing" love to those who others would reject.

THE PAIN OF REJECTION

Nothing can wound your heart like rejection. The most penetrating wound is the painful rejection of a loved one. Even death itself does not pierce your heart as deeply as when you know you have been abandoned. You feel devastated when someone dear to your heart deserts you. Rejection chips away at your self-image . . . chisels down your confidence . . . and challenges your hope. Meanwhile, the memory of your loved one lingers on and on in the recesses of your mind, repeating—through whispers and shouts—those haunting messages: "You are unwelcome . . . .You are unworthy." (Hopefortheheart.org/rejection)

There are overt causes of rejection like, abandonment, disapproval, divorce, humiliation, infidelity, prejudice, sexual abuse, and adoption.

There are also covert causes of rejection like, addictions, broken promises, performance-based acceptance, handicaps, comparison, death/critical illness or discrimination.

REFLECTION QUESTIONS

Think about the person in your life or family member that you struggle to accept their lifestyle or the decision they have made as you answer these questions.

Are you holding back love to a gay family member? Why?

How did Satan trick you to feel ashamed?

What behaviors did you demonstrate because of your shame?

How have you been hurtful in your words or action because of shame?

What have you felt guilty about?

What negative behavior has guilt caused?

How have you been hurtful in your words or actions because of guilt?

From Rejection to Rejoicing

Because of your hurt, how has it caused you to act towards the other person?

When you think about it, what would you do differently in the situation?

Read Proverbs 12: 18, what does it teach you about the situation?

Are your behaviors overt or covert?

Read Proverbs 15:18, what does it teach you about anger?

Read Hebrews 9:14-15, what do you learn about guilt?

When Push Comes To Love

If you could do it all over again how would you handle these emotions?

Now that you know what to do, what will be the first thing you do.

CHAPTER 2

THE FIGHT
Spiritual Warfare

THE FIGHT
Spiritual Warfare

"For we wrestle not against flesh and blood, but against principalities, against powers, against rulers of the darkness of this world against spiritual wickedness in high places."

The scripture above is where you need to start to be able to fight this battle. Once you understand the trick, it helps you with the fight. But it's not until you understand, Satan's tricks that you can truly fight fire with faith. I fought flesh and blood and my daughter took the licks. Now, please understand that it was not my "intent" to fight with her but it was the "affect." We have to look at our intentions and how they affect others even if we have good intentions they can still hurt.

As you read this chapter, remember what you are fighting for. Our goal is to get to heaven and live with God forever.

FIGHTING FLESH

From Rejection to Rejoicing

To look back, I was never going to win a spiritual battle fighting with flesh and blood. In the mist of it, I could not see the rulers of darkness and spiritual wickedness, all I could see was Jasmine.

In Mark 8:33, Jesus looked at Peter and said, "get thee behind me, Satan." He *looked* at Peter but *spoke* to Satan. Which means that Peter's action was being lead by Satan. Jesus did not attack Peter but Satan. This is a great example of fighting spiritual darkness and not flesh and blood.

My fight with Jasmine lasted for years. I knew this scripture and had heard it before but it eventually became real to me and they became more than just words on paper, in a book. I was praying and asking God to fix our relationship. To be honest, I wanted him to fix Jasmine and that would fix our relationship.

This situation caused not only fighting with my daughter but with my husband and our other kids. My husband and I were struggling through this situation. We both were Christians, but we did not know how to get through what was happening

When Push Comes To Love

in our family. He was embarrassed and ashamed too and he made it very visible to Jasmine, just like I did.

He was out of town working one day and I was at a friend's house, when I got a call from Jasmine saying the house was on fire. "What?" I screamed, "where are you now?" "I am outside," "I am on my way." I jumped in the car and rushed home. I was twenty minutes away from the house. When I got there, there were three fire trucks outside my house. I walked in and they had put the fire out and water was everywhere and they were removing all the water from the floors. When they left, I asked Jasmine, how did you start the fire, she said, "I put some grease on to cook French fries and went upstairs and I forgot about it until I started to smell the grease burning, so I ran downstairs and the skillet was burning so I threw some water on it and it blew up and caught the curtains on fire and I couldn't put it out." I was so upset. My first thought was she was on the phone with some girl and almost burnt the house down. The fire just added fuel to the fire that was already going on in our house and in our relationship.

From Rejection to Rejoicing

I called my husband to tell him what happened and he was furious with her. What I know is that if we had not been having issues with her being gay, we would have been upset but not to the extent that we were because she was gay. Like I said earlier, her being gay made everything bigger than it really was.

My husband got home and of course we got into an argument about it. We were in the room talking about it and I could see he was frustrated but I knew what extent by the words he said to me. My husband in his anger, looked at me and said, "she has to go, she needs to go live with her father." I responded, "what do you mean she has to go," I said, he said "I can't take it anymore, she keeps doing things that don't make sense, she needs to go." A mother never ever wants to hear her husband say that he wants her child to leave, especially when he is not her biological father. I said, "No, she is not going to live with her father." He knew how I felt about her living with her dad. How could he say that to me is all I could think about. Tears rolled down my face as he said, "as the man of this house, I have to do what's right for this family." I couldn't not stop crying, this was my child. As I write these words today, tears still come to my eyes. He didn't want her to leave because of the fire; he wanted her to leave because of her lifestyle.

I felt that I had to fight my husband on Jasmine's behalf, which made him feel that I was accepting what she was doing, which caused more fighting.

My husband and I were fighting so much that we decided to speak to our minister about the situation. We needed some help. During the meeting with our minister, my husband's anger was evident and at one point he said, "I shouldn't have to go through this." We were already fighting before we met with our minister because he told me, "I didn't sign up for this when we got married." I said, "What are you saying, that you want the marriage to be smooth or you want out." I was so hurt. Our marriage was on the verge of divorce because I was not going to let him mistreat her.

During our counseling session with our minister, Bro White looked at my husband and said, "why not you?" My husband looked at him like, what

From Rejection to Rejoicing

do you mean? And the minister said it again, "why not you? What makes you different than any other person that has to go through trials?" My husband couldn't say a word. Actually my husband was angry to hear that. He wanted someone on his side that he was right, but that didn't happen. We both were wrong.

I was so grateful for the conversation with our minister because he told us to look inside of ourselves to figure out what we need to learn. That went in one ear and out the other ear of my husbands. He didn't want to deal with the situation. He just wanted the little girl he knew back.

My husband fought flesh and blood a lot longer than I did and that made it even harder for our marriage.

We were fighting each other; we did not realize we were in a spiritual war.

I was praying one night and I asked God, please fix this. Then the words of Paul came to me so clearly when he said in 2 Corinthians 12:7-9,

When Push Comes To Love

"...Because of these surpassingly great revelations. Therefore, in order to keep me from becoming conceited, I was given a thorn in my flesh, a messenger of Satan, to torment me. Three times I pleaded with the Lord to take it away from me. But he said to me, My grace is sufficient for you, for my power is made perfect in weakness. Therefore I will boast all the more gladly about my weakness, so that Christ's power may rest on me."

That was it, God was not going to change Jasmine or the situation, it was me he was working on. This was a lesson that he was teaching me. Everything will not be easy, but my grace is sufficient. That was the message that I received when I read that passage of scripture at that moment.

When I realized this, another question changed my life. I asked God as I prayed, "what are you trying to teach me about me?" That was the first time that I did not make it about Jasmine but about me. This question change my life and my relationship with God and Jasmine.

From Rejection to Rejoicing

I then realized that I was in a spiritual war. You cannot fight spirit with flesh because you will never win. I had to stop fighting Jasmine and start fighting Satan. Jasmine needed love.

I believe God is working in me no matter what I may feel or how the situation may look. *"Being confident of this, that He who began a good work in me and He will bring it to full completion."* (Philippians 1:6, 2:13) There is something for you to learn during your trials and tribulations. Take your eye off the situation and look within, that's where the change starts.

I shared with my husband what God was teaching me and my husband thought that it was great but he still wasn't ready to accept Jasmine. He said over and over, that I don't have a problem with Jasmine yet he continued to distance himself from her.

He was friendly and cordial to her but that wasn't showing love. She felt it too.

He told me, I'm not where you are and you have to leave me alone about it, but I couldn't because it wasn't right how we treated her and he needed to see that. All it did was cause us to fight more.

HOW TO FIGHT

I started using the weapon of the Word to tear down my stronghold against my daughter. Below are the scriptures that I used to help me love like Christ said to love, I want to share them with you and hope you find comfort in them as I did.

- *Romans 13:8 - Owe no one anything, except to love each other, for the one who loves another has fulfilled the law. (KJV)*

- *Galatians 5:13 - For you were called to freedom, brothers. Only do not use your freedom as an opportunity for the flesh, but through love serve one another. (ESV)*

- *John 13:34-35 - A new command I give you: Love one another. As I have loved you, so you must love one another. By this everyone will know that you are my disciples, if you love one another." (NIV)*

From Rejection to Rejoicing

- *John 15:12 - My command is this: Love each other as I have loved you. (NIV)*

- *Romans 12:10 - Be devoted to one another in brotherly love. Honor one another above yourselves. (ESV)*

- *Romans 14:13 - therefore let us stop passing judgment on one another. Instead, make up your mind not to put any stumbling block or obstacle in your brother's way. (ESV)*

- *Romans 15:7 - Accept one another, then, just as Christ accepted you, in order to bring praise to God. (ESV)*

- *Ephesians 4:2 - Be completely humble and gentle; be patient, bearing with one another in love. (ESV)*

- *Ephesians 4:32 - Be kind and compassionate to one another, forgiving each other, just as in Christ God forgave you.*

When Push Comes To Love

Christian's, we must stop fighting in the literal sense homosexuals and gay people. I can see it so clear now, since my eyes have been opened through my daughter. I have talked to Christians that have family members that are gay and they have rejected them. They push and shove because Satan's has tricked them too. I get calls from people asking me, "Becky can you talk to a friend of mine, she just found out her child is gay and she's having a hard time with it."

I have talked to so many people who reacted the same way I did and I try to help them understand what they are feeling and every time, it leads to being more about *them* then their family member.

Since I have lived through it, they share more with me than they do with someone who has not had to deal with a gay family member. I realize today why, I went through this ordeal, it was because one day, God wanted me to help other Christians love through tough experiences.

The one place a homosexual or anybody for that fact should feel love is in the church with Christians. Unfortunately, that is too often not the case. In researching information for this book, and looking at how the church responds to the gay lifestyle, sadly the church does not consistently *show* love. Not all churches do this, but there are quite a few churches that turn away from people who are gay. There are some that do embrace people who are gay and show genuine love towards them.

James 1:1-3, *What causes fights and quarrels among you? Don't they come from your desires that battle within you? You want something but don't get it. You kill and covet, but you cannot have what you want. You quarrel and fight. You do not have, because you do not ask God. When you ask, you do not receive because you ask with wrong motives, that you may spend what you get on your pleasures.*

Boy was this scripture talking to me. I wanted what I wanted and in the time I wanted it. My own desires are why I fought with Jasmine.

We see gay churches forming and starting, and it is because they are usually not welcomed and shown love in a traditional Christian church.

When Push Comes To Love

The gay community feels that they are most rejected by the church than any other groups based on research. We have to learn to love the sinner, because **we** are sinners too. Unfortunately, the sin is hated along with the sinner.

In a December 2011 article in ABCnews.com, it talked about Jay Lowder, an evangelical Christian, who shunned his sister for fifteen years because she came out as a lesbian, before finally accepting her sexuality. For fifteen years his sister did not feel loved by her brother. Thank God, he finally accepted his sister and was able to love her again.

FIGHTING IN THE SPIRIT
Spiritual warfare is resisting, overcoming and defeating the lies of the enemy (lust of the eyes, lust of the flesh, pride of life) that he sends our way.

These are the weapons that Satan uses for you to fall short of God's glory. These tactics are not new. He used these on Eve in Genesis 3:1-8.

From Rejection to Rejoicing

A Christian also has weapons to use in a spiritual fight. Ephesians 6:10 -18,

Finally, be strong in the Lord and in the strength of his might. Put on the whole armor of God, that you may be able to stand against the schemes of the devil. For we do not wrestle against flesh and blood, but against the rulers, against the authorities, against the cosmic powers over this present darkness, against the spiritual forces of evil in the heavenly places. There fore take up the whole armor of God, that you may be able to withstand in the evil day, and having fastened on the belt of truth, and having put on the breast plate of righteousness, and, as shoes for your feet, having put on the readiness given by the gospel of peace. In all circumstances take up the shield of faith, with which you can extinguish all the flaming darts of the evil one; and take the helmet of salvation, and the sword of the Spirit, which is the word of God, praying at all times in the Spirit, with all prayer and supplication. To that end keep alert with all perseverance, making supplication for all the saints.

This is a portrayal of the Christian life in spiritual warfare using the Lord's resources. Paul introduces the armor of God by focusing on the strength it gives. Because Christians cannot stand on their own against superhuman powers, they must rely upon the strength of the Lord's own **might**, which he supplies chiefly through prayer.

The word whole armor refers to the complete equipment of a fully armed soldier, consisting of both shields and weapons.

Spiritual **rulers, authorities, and cosmic powers**, gives a sobering glimpse into the devil's allies, the spiritual forces of evil who are exceedingly powerful in their exercise of cosmic powers over this present darkness. And yet the scripture makes clear that the enemy host is no match for the Lord, who has "disarmed the rulers and authorities and put them to open shame, by triumphing over them in him." (Col. 2:15- Eph. 1:19-21)

Breastplate of righteousness- refers not to justification, obtained at conversion but to the sanctifying righteousness of Christ practiced in a believer's life. As a soldier's breastplate protected his chest from the enemy's attacks, so sanctifying, righteous living guards a believers heart against the assaults of the devil.

Gospel of Peace - A believer's stability or sure-footedness from the gospel that gives him peace so he can stand in the battle.

Shield - the shield in a Roman soldier's attire was made of wood. It was overlaid with linen and leather, to absorb fiery arrows. Thus it also protected the other pieces of the armor; hence Paul used the phrase, in additional to all this. **Of faith-** is a genitive of content; the shield consists of faith. The idea, then, is that a Christian's resolute faith in the Lord can stop and extinguish all the flaming arrows of the evil one aimed at him.

Helmet of Salvation - refers either to present safety from the devil's attacks or to the future deliverance, "the hope of salvation as a helmet"

The sword of the Spirit - it refers to the word of God. Believers need this "sword" to combat the enemy's assault, much as Christ did three times when temped by the devil.

Praying and being alert - when the enemy attacks-on all occasions-Christians are to pray continually in the spirit. And like reliable soldier, they are to be alert, literally, "In all persistence".

For All the saints - because Satan's spiritual warfare against Christ and the church. All means always mean all.

As a Christian, I did not have my armor on. I was too busy fighting flesh, my daughter, before realizing that I was doing it all wrong. I thank God, he loved me enough to not remove the thorn because I had to pay attention to the thorn because it would be my biggest teacher in life, and Christianity.

CHAPTER SUMMARY

Focus on the spirit. It is human nature to focus on flesh buy you have to tap into heaven's nature to focus on the spirit.

From Rejection to Rejoicing

Be careful how you fight because words hit just as hard and a brick and sometimes it hurts more than the brick.
Meditate on the using the whole armor. Petition God for his strength because your strength is too week to handle spiritual wickedness.

Draw near to God and he will draw near to you.

REFLECTIONS QUESTIONS

Think about someone you have been fighting against as you answer these questions.

Are you fighting spirit or flesh?

What do you believe God is teaching you?

What armor are you not wearing?

When Push Comes To Love

How does it affect you when you do not have your armor on?

Which tactic did Satan use on you? How? (Lust of eye, flesh or pride of life)

How many situations have you blown out of proportion because of the way you feel about the person's decision?

How can you fight in the spirit going forward?

CHAPTER 3

THE WORK

Submission to God

THE WORK
Submission to God

Matthew 16: 24 Then Jesus said to his disciples, "If anyone would come after me, he must deny himself and take up his cross and follow me."

As Christian believers, when we make the decision to follow Christ, we also are making the decision to deny ourselves. Wow, this is where the work happens and your life begins to transform. It will not be easy but it will be rewarded.

To get promoted you have to put in the work, sometimes it means late nights and long days, but so many are willing to put in the work to get the reward of the promotion. You have to do the same thing in your spiritual life except you don't get promotions you move from faith to faith and your reward is heaven. It's about growing.

Every time you experience trials and tribulations, it's preparing you for something greater.

Unfortunately God does not reveal it (something greater) to you right away. You only get it after you have learned the lesson from doing the work.

I had to repeat the scripture Matthew 16:24 over and over to get it in my head of what I was suppose to do. I will be the first to tell you, that this is difficult and requires daily focus but with God, "all" things are possible. (Matthew 19:26)

DENY YOURSELF
Submission to God requires you to understand what we talked about in the previous chapter, flesh verses spirit. To deny yourself is let God lead you.

In Matthew after Jesus had ministered to the multitude, in 4:25 it says, *"And there followed him great multitudes of people from Galilee, and from Decapolis, and from Jerusalem, and from Judaea, and from beyond the Jordan."*

People were following Jesus everywhere. Then came the Sermon on the Mount; eventually people started leaving and no longer following because Jesus was giving some expectations and actions that must be followed if you loved him. When the work became hard people departed.

Are you a follower of Christ? Everyday we have to die to our sin, our thoughts, our wants, and our plans. It's daily. Every trial is a new lesson to die to yourself and let God lead you. Yet we hold on to what we want.

We love comfort and we work to make our lives as comfortable as possible, but are you sacrificing Christ for comfort? As my previous pastor used to say, "If you can't say amen just say ouch."

We are called to take up a cross today and die to ourselves. We become hypocrites. What is a hypocrite? It's a person who puts on a false appearance of virtue, or a person who acts in contradiction to his/her stated beliefs.

I was a hypocrite because as a Christian, I talked about loving others but was not doing it in my own home because of what I did not like. I did not

From Rejection to Rejoicing

deny *me* for years when it came to the situation with my daughter and for years I was wrong.

Matthew 7:5 states, "You hypocrite, first take the plank out of your own eye, and then you will see clearly to remove the speck from your brothers eye."

Do you notice one has a plank and the other has a speck? The one doing all the talking has the plank, a huge piece of wood and the one being talked about have a small piece of wood. Jesus paints such a clear picture here for us to use as a guide. So often you get so focused on what other's are doing wrong you don't focus on what you are doing wrong. What plank do you have in your eye based on the way you are treating or mistreating a loved one or someone you care about because you are unhappy with their choice, decision or lifestyle?

Because your child, sister, brother, cousin, any family member is gay, you think your actions of anger, dislike, are ok but it's not. You believe that you are justified because of their sin to act or because they respond a certain way. You are wrong. You can be angry but the bible say's don't sin.

BE OBEDIENT

God gave the Israelites a simple principle in Exodus 15:26, obedience brings blessings, and disobedience brings judgment.

As Christians we have a duty to obey God's commands. You don't get to pick and choose which commands to follow, unfortunately so many Christian do, and I did. As we know the bible is a book of love with so many scriptures of how we should love.

You have to do the work. Philippians 2:6-8 states, "Who, being in the form of God, thought it not robbery to be equal to God: But made himself of no reputation, and took upon him the form of a servant, and was made in the likeness of men; and being found in fashion as a man, he humbled himself, and became obedient unto death, even the death of the cross."

You can get so caught up in the situation and making your point that you don't hear the other person. Jesus, who was God, humbled himself and was obedient unto death. What do you need to do to obey God's command to love?

The work is hard because it requires conscious thinking and conscious actions.

I was willing to put in the work to change and improve my relationship with my daughter. I repented and asked God to forgive me for my sins against my daughter and against him. Then it was time for me to ask my daughter to forgive me.

MY WORK

I called Jasmine and told her I needed to have a long overdue conversation with her. I shared with her how God had been working on me and I informed her I needed to say something to her. I took a deep breath and said,

"I want to apologize to you for all the things I have said to you and the things I did to you from the

When Push Comes To Love

time I found out about your lifestyle to now. I am so sorry for the hurt I have caused you and I realize that I should have handled it totally different. I did not show you how a Christian should act and for that I apologize. I did not think about your pain, just my embarrassment, shame and anger."

Tears fell down my face as I confessed my sins to her and asked her to forgive me. She was silent, and did not know what was going on with me. I told her that I need to ask her something and I needed her to be open and honest with me because I needed to hear it and she said, "ok mom." I asked her if she could share with me things that I have done or said that hurt her. I wanted to know but at the same time I was scared to hear her response. I braced myself and she began. She told me of several things that hurt her. She said, "I just wanted you to love me, you did not have to accept my lifestyle but I didn't think you would stop loving me." Tears continued to fall down my face as I heard her pain, pain that I had caused. She then told me, *"Mom one day you were so mad at me that you said, I don't know why I had you. I was so hurt that I cried and*

From Rejection to Rejoicing

I just wanted stay away, so that I wouldn't hurt you."

I didn't remember ever saying those words to her, but in my anger at that time, I very well could have and probably did say them. I didn't remember, but I didn't tell her that I didn't remember and I didn't try to justify it because it would have taken away from what I was trying to do, mend our relationship. The fact that she remembered each word five years later meant that I said them. I had given her a memory and a pain to carry around for four almost five years. The thought of that hurt me to my soul. I told her how sorry I was for having her carry that burden all those years. We both cried that day. We talked for several hours on the phone; it was a relief for both of us and the beginning of a new relationship of love.

My last words to her was, "Jasmine, I promise going forward that I will show you how much I love you and I will replace all those bad memories with new loving memories." I meant every word I said and I have worked to build a new relationship

When Push Comes To Love

with my daughter and I continue to work on a loving relationship with her.

Of course you know that when you want to do good, evil is always present. I was learning to get past myself and love my daughter, when I got a call from one of my relatives and asked me had I seen Jasmines hair cut, this as a couple of years later of us working on our relationship. I told them no, but then I started looking on Facebook to see if I could find a picture. When I saw the picture, I was shocked. Jasmine has had long hair all her life and hated to get it trimmed, let alone cut. When I saw that she had cut her hair like my son's, a short low fade cut, tears rolled down my face, and I thought, why.

We were working on our relationship and then I saw her hair. It hurt me, but I prayed and said, Satan, I know your tricks. You are trying to get me upset with her and I will not let you win.

I was going to visit her in a couple of months so seeing the picture prepared me to be ready when I saw her in person. I realized that seeing the picture first was God preparing me so that I wouldn't get upset or angry when I say her face to face.

I continued to pray and ask God for strength and to let me just love. I made a decision to not focus on her hair and to focus on my time with her. Satan knew my hot buttons and he was trying to push them with thoughts in my head and about what other people will think, but I did not give in to those thoughts. God had given me strength and I was conscious and aware, so I could make a choice of how to behave when I saw her.

You can mend broken hearts and relationships; it just requires you to put in the work.

Proverbs 3:5-6, "Trust in the Lord with all your heart and lean not to your own understanding, but in all your ways acknowledge Him and He will direct your paths." This scripture really helped me. I kept trying to understand why and I wanted to make sense of it and I could not.

My advice to you, stop trying to understand their choice or lifestyle because you will not, and it will drive you crazy. The scripture tells to lean not to

When Push Comes To Love

your understanding. You have to acknowledge God and let him direct you in your thinking and actions.

I knew when I went to visit her that I was going to meet her mate for the first time and she was excited for me to meet her and I wasn't as excited.

I decided to fast and pray prior to my going to visit her because I knew that I was going to need God's help to make it through. I went into my quiet place and meditated to gain strength from the all mighty.

When I got to her place and she met me downstairs with her friend, eager to introduce me to her. I hadn't seen Jasmine in a while so I hugged her and kissed her then she introduce me to her. I greeted her and hugged her and I said "hello, nice to meet you."

We all went to dinner and as we sat and ate, I realized that she was a really nice person. She was respectful and courteous. I didn't have any anger in my heart not did I get mad or hurt. I knew it was the God. I realized that this was the work that God expects of us as Christians. I had come a long way from where I used to be. I would have never met her or wanted to be around her a few years earlier, that's how I knew it was the God in me.

I've had people say; the bible says to depart from them, (sinner). The scripture they use is Matthew 18:15-17, *"If your brother or sister sins, go and point out their fault, just between the two of you. If they listen to you, you have won them over. But if they will not listen, take one or two others along, so that every matter may be established by the testimony of two or three witnesses. If they still refuse to listen, tell it to the church, and if they refuse to listen even to the church, treat them as you would a pagan or tax collector."*

There are other bible versions that use, "treat them like a heathen man, publican or Gentile."

These are people that were not liked and shunned by Christians and religious people in the bible days. These people had bad reputations in the community.

When Push Comes To Love

Too many people (Christians) believe that scripture means they have the right to disconnect with others.

Now let me share some other scriptures with you, Matthew 11:19, "The Son of Man came eating and drinking, and they say, "Here a glutton and a drunkard, a friend of tax collectors (publicans) and sinners. But wisdom is proved right by her deeds."

This scripture is referring to Jesus because he ate and drank with publicans, the people that the others discarded. Jesus took the time to seek and save the lost, because in His eyes, you and I are worth it all!

The wisdom of God was present in Christ as he sat and ate with the heathens. All her children, (wisdom) in contrast to the rejection by the foolish critics, prove wisdom right. Spiritually wise persons could see the ministry of Jesus was Godly. (Luke 7:35)

We have to seek that same spiritual wisdom, which is more powerful than natural wisdom.

From Rejection to Rejoicing

They called Jesus names because ate and drank with publican, and sinners but Jesus wasn't worried about what they thought about him. That's where I was wrong. I was so worried about what others would say about me, especially what Christian would say.

When I learned this about Jesus, it was a huge help to me to put in the work of love.

Jesus chose Matthew, the publican as a disciple, an apostle. (Matthew 11:19) This was someone who was looked down on from religious people, so what did Jesus see? Jesus told Levi, a publican, "follow me," Levi gets up leave his tax table and goes with Jesus. The Pharisees (religious people) were upset at Jesus' actions. They asked the disciples," Why does he eat with tax collectors and sinners?"

On hearing this, Jesus said to them, "It is not the healthy who need a doctor, but the sick. I have not come to call the righteous, but the sinner." (Luke 7:27-32)
Jesus ate and talked with people who were religious and social outcast.

We (Christians), not all Christians but too many of us, including me, don't follow Jesus' example to seek those that are lost, it's easier to just wash your hands and be done with them. To love is to work.

The person, who forgives a little, loves a little. When I forgave, my love increased. Do your work and watch God work.

CHAPTER SUMMARY

It's time to stop talking and start walking as a Christian. You have to do the heavy lifting, which requires you to repent for what you have done and ask God to forgive you. Then you have to take the next step, which is to ask the person to forgive you too for all that you have done or said.

Deny yourself. It's time to get past how you feel, what you believe is right or what you believe is wrong and do the work of LOVE.

REFLECTION QUESTIONS

What work do you need to do right now to mend a broken relationship?

When will you do the work?

What do you learn from Matthew 6:15, Mark 11:25?

If you have sinned against someone, read 1 John 1:9.

What example did Jesus show us in Luke 5:27-32)

When Push Comes To Love

What are you commanded to do in Matthew 18:21-22?

Take some time to pray and ask God to help you do the work that He intends you to do.

Chapter 4

The Change
Spirits Comfort

The Change
Spirits Comfort

John 14: But the Comforter, which is the Holy Ghost, whom the Father will send in my name, he shall teach you all things, and bring all things to your remembrance, whatsoever I have said unto you.

Now it's time for you to change. If you have not been living the commandment to love to all, it's time. You can't think about what the other person should do and how much they have hurt you; you must focus on doing what God has commanded you to do as a Christian, LOVE.

Change is not easy and never has been and never will be but it is the one constant in the world. I Corinthians 13:1-3, says, *"If I speak with tongues of men and of angels, but do not have love I have become a noisy gong or a clanging cymbal. If I have the gift of prophesy, and know all mysteries and all knowledge; and if I have all faith, so as to remove mountains, but do not have love I am nothing. And if I give all my possessions to feed the poor, and if I surrender my body to be burned, but do not have love, it profits me nothing."*

Can you see the importance of love? Now, let's be clear on love. In your heart you have not stopped loving the individual but remember there is a difference in showing love outwardly towards another person. To say you love her but not show her the love means you are not congruent in words and actions. Love changes things not only for the other person but for you too. Your relationship with God becomes closer because God *is* love. You are being god-like when you love.

REJOICING

I was ready for the change. My relationship had been strained for too long and I missed my daughter. I knew that I needed to fix it and change my actions.

One of the hardest things to do is to look at yourself and not like what you see. My change started when I stared looking at me and took all my focus off Jasmine. I am so glad that God loved me enough to force me to look at myself. If I had not, I would have never seen my actions and I would have continued to hurt Jasmine.

Please understand that God changed me and I was open to the change. I was seeking the change.

My husband did not experience the change for a couple of years after me.

I prayed and asked God to open his heart. Jasmine and I had had several conversations and she wanted the step-dad she had before all this happened. She really missed him. I told him that he needed to talk to her and work on their relationship and he kept saying, "I'm ok, Jasmine and I don't have a problem." I knew that wasn't true because of my conversations with her. I knew he wasn't ready and that he still struggled to love in spite of.

I told him, "You don't know how she feels because you have avoided talking to her about how she feels."

From Rejection to Rejoicing

She was coming to visit us one July with the rest of my family and he said that he would talk to her and let her know that he doesn't have a problem with her. He had said that he would talk to her the last time she visited but he didn't. He didn't know how so he avoided it and made up excuses why saying things like, "we did get a chance, or it was so much going on."

When she got there, I was determined for them to talk so I asked her, "Are you ready to talk to him," and she said yes. I told her, "be honest with him and let him know how you feel and what you have shared with me."

We went upstairs and I called him in to talk to her. I sat and listened as he started the conversation. He said, "Jasmine, I don't have a problem with you, but it's hard for me to accept what you are doing but I want you to know I love you."

Jasmine looked at him and said, "I know that you don't agree with my choice, but all I ever wanted you to do was what you used to do with me, like take me to breakfast, eat dinner together and just love me, not my life, just me." She continued on

When Push Comes To Love

and said, "When I left and went to my dads, I use to ask him to go eat breakfast and he would say, there food in the kitchen, but I had gotten used to our breakfast dates and I realized how much I missed them. I know you are not my dad but I see you as my dad too, and I feel your distance from me. A tear fell down her face as she asked, "I just want you to love me like you would any human being, that's all I ask, I don't expect you to accept my life but I did expect you to love me."
I could see he was shocked by her words. He did not realize how important he was in her life and how much she missed him. He did not know her hurt from his distance in love towards her.

I could see his heart soften in that moment. He reached over and hugged her and of course, I cried. God had changed our lives and our relationships.

He promised her that going forward he would show love to her and he apologized to her for making her feel that way.

God was present in our house that day and it was evident. It was one of the greatest times that we had with Jasmine in a long time as a family. I watched him hug her, something he hadn't done in a long time. I watched her smile like the little girl inside her was happy.

My respect for my husband increased in that instance. God had touched his heart. Our marriage grew stronger because the issue with his rejection of her causes problems in our marriage. That day was a day of rejoicing.

Feeling love is important to every human being. We all want to be love.

Because my relationship with my daughter is the best it's ever been today and her relationship with my husband is stronger, I rejoice. The joy of the Lord is my strength.

FIND COMFORT IN THE SCRIPTURES

I found comfort in the word of God. His word is true and I needed to believe and have faith in his word. These are scriptures that ministered to me and helped me with my thoughts and relationship.

- *Ephesians 3:20 Now unto Him who is able to do exceedingly abundantly above all that we ask or think, according to the power that works in us. (KJV)*

I found comfort here because God can do much more that I ask. I asked him specific prayers and I believe that he will answer them. I have to tap into the power he has given me. I wasn't using my power but expecting the scripture to work.

Do you just read the first part of the scripture and overlook the latter part of it? You have to believe you have *power*.

- *… Call those things, which are not as though they were. Romans 4:17B.*

I had to speak in the now and the future and get my thoughts out of the past. You have to believe in God's power to heal.

- *Rejoice in the Lord always; again I say, rejoice! Let your gentle spirit be known to all men. The Lord is near. Be anxious for nothing, but in everything by prayer and supplication with thanksgiving let your requests be made know to God. And the peace of God will surpass all comprehension; will guard your hearts and your minds in Christ Jesus. Phil. 4:4-7*

This was one that helped because I was so anxious to move beyond this phase and stage with Jasmine. I had to learn to rejoice, then to be gentle. The scripture is true because I started to experience peace. I stopped worrying about her changing because I gave it all to God.

Sometimes the trials and pressures of life make it almost impossible to be happy. But Paul did not tell readers to be happy. He encouraged us to rejoice in the Lord. In fact, he said it twice.

- *Consider it pure joy, my brothers and sisters when you face trials of many kinds because you know that the testing of your faith produces perseverance. Let perseverance finish it work so that you may be mature and complete, not lacking anything. If any of you lacks wisdom, you should ask God, who gives generously to all without finding fault, and it will be given to you. James 2:2-5*

The scripture starts with seeing trials as joy. I didn't get it at first, I had to meditate and pray on this scripture to really understand how to count trials as joy. I started to practice the joy and the more joy I had the more I could deal with. I earnestly prayed for wisdom and God gave freely the wisdom to understand the situation better.

- *But when you ask, you must believe and not doubt, because the one who doubts is like a wave of the sea blown and tossed by the wind. That person should not expect to receive anything from the Lord. James 2:6-7*

Here is where my eyes were opened. We ask God all the time to change our situations and outcomes. We ask him to fix our relationships but how often to we believe that he will do it? I asked but thought I needed to help God to fix the relationship and each time I made it worse.

When I realized that I needed to believe God, I asked God to forgive me for my non-belief. I changed the way I thought about my relationship with my daughter. How could I expect God to fix, when I didn't trust him to do it? The light bulb went off in my head and I realized that I needed to increase my faith and believe. I truly believe with all my heart that God will bring my daughter out and that's where my peace comes from.

These are some of the scriptures where God spoke to me and into my situation as a mother and most importantly as a Christian.

I share them with you because maybe they can comfort you the same way they comforted me during tough times.

Spend time in the word of God and let God speak to you. The bible is full of comfort from God. It's a book of love. The more time you spend with God the better you become. God comforts us, which helps us to work on internal change.

CHAPTER SUMMARY

Take comfort in the word of God. When you can't He can. Lean on his everlasting arms.

Your light must shine especially in darkness, because that light might be the difference in your relationship.

REFLECTION QUESTIONS

Find three scriptures that give you comfort?

What time of day can you commit to praying about your situation and relationship?

What comfort do you get from Proverbs 3:5-6?

From Rejection to Rejoicing

What comfort do you get from Colossians 3:12?

Sin is not ended by multiplying words, but the prudent hold their tongues. Proverbs 10:19. How does this scripture comfort you?

Chapter 5

The Challenge
Self or Savior?

―― From Rejection to Rejoicing ――

The Challenge
Self or Savior?

Then Jesus said to his disciples, "Whoever wants to be my disciple must deny themselves and take up their cross and follow me. – Matthew 16:24 NIV

What's more important to you, self or the savior? That was a question that I had to ask myself. If you have missed it, this is a book about love. Too often when we have disagreements or dislike someone's choices, we shove our ideas, thoughts and beliefs down their throats when we should focus on how we show love, even when we disagree.

As Christians our lives should be a life of love towards others.

1 Corinthians 13:1-3

"If I speak with the tongues of men and of angels but do not have love, I have become a noisy gong or a clanging cymbal. If I have a the gift of prophecy, and know all mysteries and all knowledge; and if I have all faith, so to remove

mountains, but do not have love, I am nothing. And If I give all my possessions to feed the poor, and if I surrender my body to be burned, but do not have love, it profits me nothing."

It's time to change relationships from, "when push comes to shove," to when push comes to LOVE." This is the expectation of God for all Christians.

This is my story and my experience. I have opened and bared my soul in an effort to help you build a stronger relationship with a friend, loved one or family member. It was difficult to write this book and it was emotional to revisit some bad memories, but because of my LOVE for you, it was worth it, especially if it helps you improve the way you LOVE.

This book is a labor of love. I realize that my experience with my daughter was for me to help as many Christians as I can, to show love. When I focused on LOVE our relationship changed and I grew spiritually.

There will be some who do not agree with this book or me and that's ok. We can agree to disagree and still act in love. This is my experience and no one can change what God has shown me or what God has revealed to me during this time of my life. I thank Him for the experience. It's time to start a conversation with Christians about how we love when we don't like.

I have messed up so many times but I know that God still loves me. It's humbling to me and it amazes me how much He loves me with all my faults. I shed tears as I think about His love.

If you know someone who is having a tough time with a relationship with someone who is gay, share this book and pray that God opens there heart to love unconditionally.

God wants to use you to share his message and to build the kingdom of God. He can use anyone, even me to share my story to help others. No one is perfect, but God can use an imperfect person to share a perfect message. Look at his record of the people he used that were not perfect:

Noah was a drunk

When Push Comes To Love

Abraham was too old
Isaac was a daydreamer
Jacob was a liar
Leah was ugly
Joseph was abused
Moses had a stuttering problem
Gideon was afraid
Samson had long hair and was a womanizer
Rahab was a prostitute
Jeremiah and Timothy were too young
David had an affair and was a murderer
Elijah was suicidal
Isaiah preached naked
Jonah ran from God
Naomi was a widow
Job went bankrupt
John the Baptist ate bugs
Peter denied Christ
The Disciples fell asleep while praying
Martha worried about everything
The Samaritan woman was divorced, more than once
Zaccheus was too small
Paul was too religious
Timothy had an ulcer...
AND Lazarus was dead!

Just think how he can use you by the love you show to someone else.

THE CHALLENGE

Now it's time to take the challenge. The hardest thing to do is apply what you know by taking action. When you go to church and the message was great, how often do you decide that the message was great enough to change how you do things? Application is one of the hardest things for most people. That's why this will be a challenge for you.

Until you do the work, Satan will continue to keep your thoughts focused on his tricks. It's time to take responsibility for your actions, and not the actions of someone else. When you stand before God, there will be no one there but YOU to give an account of your life.

Here is the challenge. For twelve weeks you will be given a *LOVE PUSH* challenge to set aside ten to fifteen minutes a day to meditate and pray on a specific scripture, take action then journal

When Push Comes To Love

your day. Focus on the relationships you need to mend, the people you need to forgive and your relationship with God. Move closer to Him and He will move closer to you. In the quiet moments you can hear Him clearly. Use these weekly love push challenges to listen. It will change your life and the life of the people you love.

James 1:22-25 - *Do not merely listen to the word, and so deceive yourselves. Do what it says. Anyone who listens to the worked but does not do what it says is like a man who looks at his face in a mirror and after looking at himself, goes away and immediately forgets what he looks like. But the man, who looks intently into the perfect law that gives freedom, and continues to do this, is not forgetting what he has heard but doing it--he will be blessed in what he does. (NIV)*

What's more important, self or savior? Your actions will reveal your decision.

From Rejection to Rejoicing

90-Day Love Push Challenge
(12 weeks)

"Patience is where love meets wisdom."

— Love Dare

WEEK 1

Push Patience
Love is Patient... - I Corinthians 13-3

Patience is bearing of provocation, annoyance, misfortune, or pain, without complaint, loss of temper, irritation or the like.

I Thessalonians 5:14, And I urge you, brothers, warn those who are idle, encourage the timid, help the weak, be patient with everyone.

When you are patient you are making a choice to respond positively to a negative situation. Patience shows that Christians are following God's plan and timetable rather than there own and that they have abandoned their own ideas about how the world should work.

We don't listen patiently but if you are wise you understand that patience is essential to building strong relationships. Patient is a journey and not a destination, so you will be faced with it over and over.

Without patience expect wars.

THIS WEEKS PRAYER

Lord give me patience today. Help me to listen to hear, and speak to heal. Give me your strength
to pass the test of patience. Lord if I fail, give me the opportunity to fix it. Let me have the patience that you gave Job to hold on and with stand.

THIS WEEKS AFFIRMATION

I am patient with the people and things that I am against or disagree with.

PUSH LOVE CHALLENGE

This week, focus on patience. What action can you take to demonstrate patience to the friend or family member? Demonstrate patience through listening without judging.

From Rejection to Rejoicing

___ Did you complete today's challenge.

What was difficult about patience? What did you do for this challenge and what was the outcome?

_____

_____

_____

_____

_____

_____

_____

_____

When Push Comes To Love

From Rejection to Rejoicing

"It is pride that
changed
angels into devil's;
it was
humility that makes
men
as angles."
—St. Augustine

WEEK 2
Push Away Pride
Pride comes before destruction - Proverbs 16:18

Pride is a high or inordinate opinion of one's own dignity, importance, merit or superiority, whether as cherished in the mind or as displaying in bearing or conduct.

Pride leads to one's downfall and brings about contention. Proverbs 28:25 says, *"He that is of a proud heart stirs up strife: but he that puts his trust in the Lord shall be made fat."* To live a life of love one must put away pride. The opposite of pride is humility. A common cause of anger is pride.

Usually you don't want anyone to know what you are dealing with in your family, so you let pride keep you silent. We all have struggles and deal with trials and tribulations yet we act like everything is all right all the time.

THIS WEEKS PRAYER

Lord, please endow me with humility today.
As I go through this day, give me the strength
to fight against my prideful nature. Lord, if I display
acts of pride bring it to my attention so that I may
correct my behavior.

THIS WEEKS AFFIRMATION

I am full of humility.

From Rejection to Rejoicing

PUSH LOVE CHALLENGE

This week focus on removing pride. Don't let the evil one fill you with prideful thoughts and actions. Push for humility

___ Did you complete today's challenge?

What conversation stimulated prideful responses? What are you ashamed of that causes pride to creep in?

_____

_____

_____

_____

_____

When Push Comes To Love

> "You can live in peace or in pieces."
>
> -Iyanla Vanzant

WEEK 3

Push Peace

And let the peace of God rule in your hearts, to which also ye are called in one body; and be ye thankful.
-Colossians 3:15

Peace refers to a state of being mentally and spiritually. Being at peace is healthy and it's the opposite of being stressed or anxious. Peace is the product of God having reconciled sinners to him, so that they are no longer enemies, which should result in confidence and freedom in approaching God.

Peace is one of the fruits of the spirit in Galatians 5:22. Life is difficult and at time seems unfair. Events almost never turn out exactly as planned so it's understandable why we all want tranquility. We have to learn to be peacemakers and not peace-breakers.

It takes two to argue but it only takes one to bring peace. Show your love through being a peacemaker.

From Rejection to Rejoicing

THIS WEEKS PRAYER

Lord, help me sow the seed of peace today. Where there is
hurt and pain all around, let me lead peace with others. Give me peace of mind to accept the things that I cannot change. Rain down drops of peace on me today.

THIS WEEKS AFFIRMATION

I am a peacemaker and calm in my communication.

When Push Comes To Love

PUSH LOVE CHALLENGE

This week focus on being a peacemaker in your thoughts,
actions and communication. When you start to feel
angry or upset, focus on peace and prayer.

___ Did you complete the todays challenge?

What happen this week that tested your peace?
How did you make peace today? Share your day.

_____

_____

_____

_____

_____

From Rejection to Rejoicing

When Push Comes To Love

WEEK 4

From Rejection to Rejoicing

Push Goodness

Most men will proclaim everyone his own goodness;
but a faithful man who can find? -Proverbs 20:6

Goodness means working for the benefit of others, not oneself. Goodness may be thought of both as an uprightness of soul and as an action reaching out to others to do good even when it is not deserved.

Romans 15:14 provides a clear sense of goodness: "Now I myself am confident concerning you, my brethren, that you also are full of goodness, filled with all knowledge, able also to admonish one another." Paul links goodness with full knowledge and admonition of each other. This gives us insight into what he knew of and expected from Christians in Rome, placing before us a target shoot for in our relationships.

THIS WEEKS PRAYER

When Push Comes To Love

Lord, help me to demonstrate your goodness in my thoughts, words and actions today. Let me represent who you are by the way I show goodness towards others.

THIS WEEKS AFFIRMATION

I am goodness in the eyes of Jesus Christ.

PUSH LOVE CHALLENGE

This week focus is the goodness of God. As you interact
with others and the loved ones lifestyle, reveal God's
goodness through love.

__ Did you complete todays challenge

From Rejection to Rejoicing

What did you do to show goodness today? Did you have any obstacles to overcome?

_____
_____
_____
_____
_____
_____
_____
_____
_____
_____
_____

When Push Comes To Love

From Rejection to Rejoicing

"Nothing is as strong as gentleness, nothing so gentle as real strength"

-St. Frances de Sales

WEEK 5

Push Gentleness

Gentleness and self-control, against such things there is no law. Gal 5:23

Philippians 4:5 Paul says, Let your gentleness be evident to all. The Lord is near. Gentleness is also referred to as meekness, which means, forbearance, mildness. Gentleness and meekness is inward grace of the soul, calmness toward God in particular. It is the acceptance of God's dealings wit us considering them as good in that they enhance the closeness of our relationship with him.

Gentleness is a quality Jesus attributes to himself in Matthew 11:29 - *Take my yoke upon you, and learn of me; for I am meek (gentle) and lowly in heart; and ye shall find rest for your souls.* It takes strength to be gentle. Don't mix up weakness with meekness they mean two totally different things.

When Push Comes To Love

THIS WEEKS PRAYER

Lord, give me the gentleness of Jesus. Let me show your strength through my gentleness. Help me to demonstrate this fruit of your spirit today.

THIS WEEKS AFFIRMATION

I am gentle in my word and actions.

PUSH LOVE CHALLENGE

This weeks focus on the spirit of gentleness and meekness.
Let it show up in all that you do. It is a gift from God and you imitate Christ when you are gentle.

From Rejection to Rejoicing

____ Did you complete todays challenge?

How did you demonstrate gentleness in your relationships? What tried to stop you from being gentle? Journal your challenge.

_____

_____

_____

_____

_____

_____

_____

_____

When Push Comes To Love

From Rejection to Rejoicing

"Love saves lives and relationships."

-Becky A. Davis

WEEK 6
Push Self-Control

For the flesh lusts against the spirit, and the Spirit against the flesh: and these are contrary the one to the other: so that you cannot do the things that you would.
Galatians 5:17

Self-control is the discipline given by the Holy Spirit that allows Christians to resist the power of the flesh. Our flesh is ego driven and ego is all about you. Ego focuses you on pleasing you. It has been said that ego stands for edging God out.

It is when we edge God out and exhaust ourselves that we get into trouble. We create the trouble because we do not exercise our gift of the holy spirit of self-control.

Self-control is about self-mastery in curbing the fleshy impulses we face. You cannot obtain this quality apart from God.

THIS WEEKS PRAYER

Lord, grant me the ability to control my thoughts, words and actions. As I face the challenges
of the day, let your word appear in my spirit to keep me focused on you. Help me die daily to my flesh.
Let me show love through self-control.

THIS WEEKS AFFIRMATION

I am a person of great self-control no matter what situation I face.

PUSH LOVE CHALLENGE

This weeks focus on controlling yourself. As you interact
with your loved one, focus on denying fleshly impulses.

From Rejection to Rejoicing

Ask for forgiveness if you lose control immediately.

____ Did you complete todays challenge?

How did you demonstrate self-control today? Did your ego get in the way?

Journal your experiences.

_____

_____

_____

_____

_____

_____

When Push Comes To Love

From Rejection to Rejoicing

When Push Comes To Love

WEEK 7
Push Forgetting
...and it keeps no record of being wronged.
I Corinthians 13:5

Love keeps no record of being wronged. Jesus carried a cross up a rugged hill while being hit, pushed and even stones were thrown. He had his hands nailed then his feet to the cross. He was stabbed in the side. A crown of thorns was put on his head and he was left to die; yet as he looked at his abusers and accusers he said, *"Father forgive them for they know not what they do."* That is an example of continuing to love and not keeping a record of wrongs.

We struggle with this when people have hurt us. It is the war of spirit against flesh. Love is able to let go and move on and it brings healing to the relationship.

THIS WEEKS PRAYER

Lord, help me to forgive those who

When Push Comes To Love

have done wrong towards me. Let me follow your example on the cross of love. Keep me from bringing up things in the past that are hurtful to me and to others. I need to get past those things with your help.

THIS WEEKS AFFIRMATION

I am forgiving and not keeping score anymore of the pain caused to me.

"Encouragement is food for the soul."
-Becky A Davis

WEEK 8

Push Encouragement

Let no corrupt communication proceed out of your mouth, but that which is good to the use of edifying,
that it may minister grace unto the hearers.

We must be careful in our communication and how we talk to the ones we love. We can hurt more than someone on the outside.

Christian must stop evil speech, substituting talk that is good for building up and giving grace. Corrupting applies to bad or rotten fruit or fish. To give grace in speaking means to benefit others rather than corrupt them through what is said.

You must learn to speak words for edification. The Holy Spirit helps to guard ones speech.

THIS WEEKS PRAYER

Lord, guide my tongue today. Let no unwholesome talk

From Rejection to Rejoicing

come out of me today. Let me be a source of encouragement to my loved one. I want to drop this stone today.

THIS WEEKS AFFIRMATION

I am and encourager to my loved ones.

PUSH LOVE CHALLENGE

This week share words of encouragement in your conversations with loved ones. Refrain from words that will tear down and focus on words that will build up.

___ Did you complete todays challenge? How did you encourage your loved one today? Was it hard for you to refrain from negative conversations?

When Push Comes To Love

Journal your experience.

From Rejection to Rejoicing

When Push Comes To Love

"Imitate God and be an Inspiration"

-Becky A Davis

WEEK 9

Push Imitation

Imitate God, therefore, in everything you do, because you are his dear children
Ephesians 5:1

As a child imitates his parents, so ought a believer to imitate God. If you read the above scripture further it talks about imitating God by waling in love and to imitate holy living by your conduct.

We are called to imitate God in every aspect of our lives. Jesus was our example of how to imitate God.

Make up your mind that you are love the way God loved and if and when you fall short you will not stop trying to imitate God's love towards others.

THIS WEEKS PRAYER

Lord, let me follow your example today. I want to love the way you love, unconditionally. Help me to repeat your actions throughout my day. When I am faced with a challenge, I want to imitate you.

THIS WEEKS AFFIRMATION

I am made in God's image and I am a spark of God.

PUSH LOVE CHALLENGE

This week resolve to be an imitator of God.
Be an example of his love in your actions.
Think about how you can make your situation better
when you imitate God.

___ Did you complete todays challenge?

Focus on your relationship and how you can reveal God though your actions today. How did you imitate God? What was the response or reaction?

When Push Comes To Love

Journal your experience.

_____

_____

_____

_____

_____

_____

_____

_____

_____

_____

From Rejection to Rejoicing

When Push Comes To Love

"Division is Satan's plan, unity is God's."

Becky A Davis

WEEK 10

Push Unity

Make every effort to keep the unity
of the Spirit through the bond of peace
Ephesians 4:3

God produced unit through the reconciling death of Christ. It is the heavy responsibility of Christians to keep that unity from being disturbed.

The trinity is an excellent example of unity. All three work together. Unity is a reflection of love. What would happen if you made it your business to do everything possible to promote unity of heart with your loved one? What would become of that relationship?

THIS WEEKS PRAYER

Lord, please reveal to me anything in my heart that is threatening the oneness with my loved one. Lord, I am asking you to help me

From Rejection to Rejoicing

build unity with my loved one.

THIS WEEKS AFFIRMATION

I am building unity with my relationships.

PUSH LOVE CHALLENGE

This week, focus on one area you could bring unity to your relationship. Think about the unity that Christ has with the church and the unity of the trinity in your actions.

___ Did you complete todays challenge?

Pick one area of division that you want to focus on bridging unity with your loved one. How will you start building unity?

When Push Comes To Love

Journal your experiences.

_____

_____

_____

_____

_____

_____

_____

_____

_____

_____

_____

From Rejection to Rejoicing

"Everyone wants transformation but no one wants to change."

WEEK 11
Push Long-Suffering

> I beseech you that you walk worthy of the Vocation wherewith you are called, with all lowliness and meekness, with longsuffering, forbearing one another in love.
> Ephesians 4:1-2

Longsuffering is also referred to as patience. Patience is being mild, gentle, and constant in all circumstances. The real test of longsuffering is not waiting, but in how one acts while he or she is waiting. A person who has developed longsuffering will be able to put up with things without losing his or her temper. Scripture tells us in James 1:4 "But let patience have her perfect work, that you may be perfect and entire, wanting nothing." Reaching this point is definitely a process, which takes a lot of practice.

When Push Comes To Love

THIS WEEKS PRAYER

Lord, help me to understand how to be patient. When I get frustrated and think I can't take anymore, give me your strength to carry one. Keep my thoughts on you. Help me to act in accordance to your word.

THIS WEEKS AFFIRMATION

God has given me the ability to be strong during my time of suffering.

PUSH LOVE CHALLENGE

This week focus on not putting time limits and what you want to happen. Think about how Christ suffered as he carried the cross, was beaten, spit on and pierced in the side and yet he suffered so that you could live.

__ Did you complete this weeks challenge?

From Rejection to Rejoicing

Was it tough to be patient in your pain? Did you show love during the tough times? Give an example.

Journal your experience.

_____

_____

_____

_____

_____

_____

_____

_____

When Push Comes To Love

WEEK 12
Push Faith

Therefore I say unto you, what things soever ye desire, when you pray, believe that you receive Them, and you shall have them.
Mark 11:24

Faith is a gift and also a manifestation of the fruit of the spirit. The gift of faith is imparted from God through the Word, but the fruit of faith is produced by the Holy Spirit. The gift of faith can move mountains, but the fruit of faith is what is required for daily living.

The fruit of faith enables us to walk and live by faith (Romans 5:2). Without this kind of faith, it is impossible to please God. (Hebrews 11:6).

Being faithful is not always easy; it requires making a decision then sticking to it no matter what regardless of what our feeling tell us. However when we are faithful and do what God tells us to do, we will be rewarded; for the Bible says that if were faithful over little things, God will make us rulers over much.

THIS WEEKS PRAYER

Lord, I know my faith get weak, forgive me for not believing the way I should. Help me to grow spiritually from faith to faith. I understand the testing of faith produces patience and I thank you for shaping and molding me into the Christian you would have me to be. Let my faith be evident to you.

THIS WEEKS AFFIRMATION

I am faithful and I am going in faith daily.

PUSH LOVE CHALLENGE

This week focus on your faith. Be aware when you faith is weak and pray. Ask God to you're your relationship and believe that He will do it.

From Rejection to Rejoicing

How aware were you when your faith became weak? Pick an area where you struggle to have faith. How will you improve your faith in that area?

Journal your experience.

_____
_____
_____
_____
_____
_____
_____
_____
_____
_____
_____
_____
_____

When Push Comes To Love

CLOSING-CONTACT US

I pray that this book has opened your heart and mind and that love has filled both. If you or someone you know has struggled with a relationship like I did, please reach out to me at www.jesusheir.com using the contact page.

SPEAKING/WORKSHOPS
I am available to speak to church groups, church events or public events and teach these principles to people who struggle in this area. I will teach

- The Trick
- The Fight
- The Work
- The Change
- The Challenge

This is a great way to start the discussion of how to love through tough times and in unpleasant situations.

I also do workshops and they are very interactive and they help you start the process of doing your work on building relationships.

You can contact me at www.jesusheir.com or email becky@jesusheir.com or call 855-639-5378

JOIN THE CONVERSATION

You are invited to join the Push Comes to Love conversation and share your thoughts, comments and questions at www.jesusheir.com/push-comes-to-love.html

T-SHIRTS at www.jesusheir.com

When you stop shoving in your relationships and seek to mend broken relationships, you have earned your push comes to love shirt.

If you know someone who has demonstrated love in a tough relationship, give a when push comes to love t-shirt.

— From Rejection to Rejoicing —

PICTURES OF JASMINE AND ME

When Push Comes To Love

From Rejection to Rejoicing

I thank God everyday for this relationship. I love her with all my heart. Satan tried to destroy us, but God is a God that mends broken relationships.

I am so proud that God blessed me with this young lady as my child. I see so much of me in her and it make's me smile.

The power of love.

From rejection to rejoicing.

ABOUT THE AUTHOR

Becky A. Davis is married to Willie Davis. They have been married for 12 years. They have four adult children, Cara, Jasmine, Cristopher and Courtney.

Becky worked in corporate America for over 20 years and was a regional vice president before starting her own business.

As an certified small business with certifications as MBE, WBE AND SBE she works as a consultant and coach to small business owners on business planning, business growth and revenue building and with corporate clients on leadership development, team building, emotional intelligence and employee engagement. Her company name is, M.V.P.work, which stands for Meaning, Values and Purpose Work. You can go to www.mvpwork.com to learn more.

She is the founder of Jesusheir LLC a Christian T-shirt apparel on-line store that teaches discipleship training designed to build up the body of Christ. www.jesusheir.com

She is also focused on giving back through her 501c3, non-profit business called Leading In High Heels, which is a charity focused on helping women of domestic violence and abuse. Heels is an acronym, Healing, Elevating, Entrusting, Love to my Sister. Go to www.leadinginhighheels.com to learn more.

From Rejection to Rejoicing

Love lifted me.
–Becky A. Davis

———— When Push Comes To Love ————

What will it do for you?

THE ~~END~~ *BEGINNING*

Made in the USA
Charleston, SC
24 March 2014